Sticky Situations

How to Get Through Them

Edited by Lauren Barnholdt

Discovery Girls, Inc.

CALIFORNIA

Discovery Girls, Inc.
445 South San Antonio Rd, Ste. 205
Los Altos, California 94022

Sticky Situations: How to Get Through Them
Copyright © 2012 Discovery Girls, Inc.
An earlier version of this book was published in 2007 as the *Fab Girls' Guide to Sticky Situations.*

This book is not intended to replace the opinions or recommendations of the reader's parents, teachers, or other experts or professionals on any of the subjects presented herein. Information, suggestions, and advice in this book are provided solely for the entertainment and as a resource to the reader and are based on research available at the time of publication. The reader should address her individual questions or concerns to her parents, teachers, counselors, physician, and other professionals and experts.

Sticky situation illustrations by Bill Tsukuda.

All DG Polls are from 2012 DiscoveryGirls.com.

ISBN 978-1-934766-05-7

Visit Discovery Girls' web site at www.discoverygirls.com.

Printed in the United States of America.

Dedication

Dedicated to the thousands of girls who have taken the time to write to Discovery Girls magazine to share your ideas, thoughts, personal stories, and yes, even your problems. All of us who work at Discovery Girls, Inc. have been deeply touched by your letters. You are a constant source of insight and inspiration, and the reason we have created this book.

Acknowledgments

I'd like to send a special thank you to all the girls who have read Discovery Girls magazine over the years and have generously shared your thoughts, ideas, and experiences with us. Without you, there would be no Discovery Girls magazine and definitely no Discovery Girls books. I feel so very fortunate to have had the opportunity to work with my dedicated and talented staff: Julia Clause, Ashley DeGree, Naomi Kirsten, Katherine Inouye Lau, Alex Saymo, Bill Tsukuda, Sarah Verney, and intern Nick Tran. Your enthusiasm and ability to keep your sense of humor while meeting insane deadlines, your willingness to work long hours, your amazing creative energy, and your insistence on always striving to get better and better have meant more to me than you will ever know—my deepest appreciation! And finally, thanks also to interns Lyn Mehe'ula and Laura Riparbelli. While every book we have published has been very much a group effort, you deserve special recognition for your creative efforts on this book; your writing talents and amazing ideas were truly essential to its creation. Your input has made all of the books so much more fun for girls to read.

Catherine Lee
PUBLISHER
DISCOVERY GIRLS

Contents

Introduction

> OH, NO!

> WHAT DO I DO NOW?

You're nearly at the bus stop on the first day of school when you suddenly stop dead in your tracks. You've just spotted your BFF. What is that green monstrosity she's wearing? "Don't you just love my outfit?!" she asks, twirling around excitedly. Your mind races as you try not to panic. Do you tell her the truth? (As in, "It's the ugliest thing I've ever seen!") Or do you tell her she looks great because...well, won't she be crushed, otherwise? It's a tough one, huh?

Not anymore! Because now you have the book that's sure to get you unstuck whenever you find yourself totally glued. We'll take you through situations from sticky...to stickier...to stickiest. What should you do if you accidentally reveal your best friend's secret crush? Or what if you're the first one in your class to wear a bra—and now you have to change for gym? Or what if you heat up your lunch in the microwave—and it catches fire? Or you overhear a conversation at school that might be about something dangerous about to go down? Never fear! The answers to all these tricky, sticky situations—and many, many more—are all right here!

This is your guide. Read it from front to back, or from back to front, or use the table of contents to find the problem you need to solve right now. However you approach it, you'll soon be an expert on getting unstuck with style. Being asked out by a boy you don't like? Regret something you said? No sweat for you...because from now on, you'll be the best-prepared girl around.

The Editors of Discovery Girls

CHAPTER ONE

When Looks Fail

Food in Teeth

You're in the cafeteria having lunch with your BFF when her crush plops his tray down at your table. "Is it okay if I sit here?" he asks, looking a little shy. You totally knew he liked her! But...uh-oh. Your BFF flashes a smile, and she has Oreos all over her teeth! "Sure," she says, still grinning, obviously unaware that she needs a toothbrush ASAP!

She's your BFF, right? Then help her! Pull your friend aside immediately! The easiest way is to say, "I really have to go to the bathroom. Can you come with me?" Once you're out of sight, she can remove the Oreos. What if your friend is too into talking with her crush to budge? In that case, whisper to her about the emergency situation without making a scene. Then she'll come with you...no matter how cute her crush is!

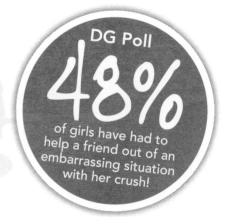

DG Poll

48%

of girls have had to help a friend out of an embarrassing situation with her crush!

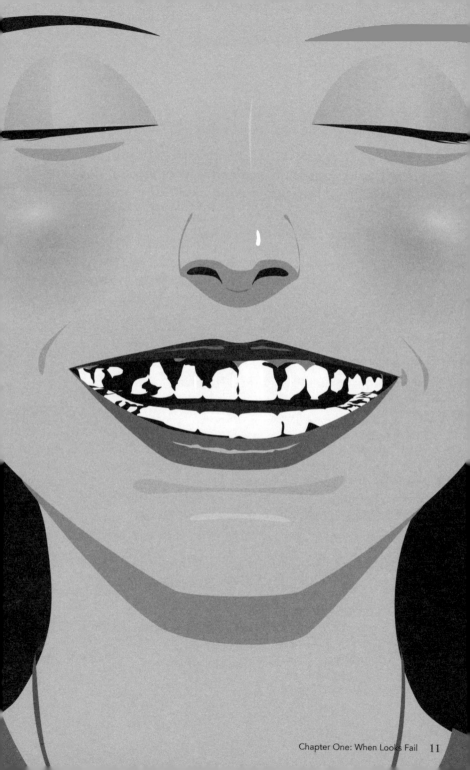

#2

Beyond Bad Hairstyle

You finally talked your mom into letting you get the new blond highlights you've been wanting forever! Unfortunately you also got the new hair stylist who didn't exactly know what she was doing...and now you're stuck with bright red streaks!

Okay, you have a big choice to make: Keep it or lose it. If you choose to keep it, work those red streaks like they were meant to be there. You have some amazing trend-setting confidence! If anyone says, "Eww, why is your hair like that?!" just proudly respond, "Why *isn't* yours?" People may respect your individuality, and it's awesome to break out from the crowd once in a while.

But if you're not feeling that brave, ask your mom to take you back to the salon, or buy an at-home hair-dye kit to return your hair to its natural color. No time to dye? Just throw on a cute bandana, headband or hat. That way, all eyes will be on your new accessory, not on your hair.

DG Poll

48% of girls have had a hair-do become a hair-don't!

SCARY HAIR!

"One day I was getting a haircut and the stylist was holding my top layer up over my head, about to cut the ends. Right as she went to snip, I shivered...and made her cut a huge chunk out of the top of my hair! At school the next day, I tried to wear a hat but my teacher made me take it off...and everybody started laughing at my mohawk!"

—Christie, age 11, N.J.

3

It's Not Pajama Day

Every December third since kindergarten has been Pajama Day at your school, and you're totally into it! This year, you wear your favorite pink footie PJs and matching pink slippers. But when you show up at school—*surprise!* Everyone's wearing their uniforms. Turns out the school cancelled Pajama Day—and you're the last one to know!

You have two choices: Either find a way to change ASAP, or embrace the fact that you're dressed for a sleepover. If you decide to change, head to the office and tell them you were unaware Pajama Day wasn't happening, and ask to call a parent to drop off some regular clothes. If you can't get in touch with your parents, tie a sweatshirt around your waist to hide your pajama pants or borrow something from a friend. If you decide not to change, just tell your classmates that you decided to hold Pajama Day anyway!

DG Poll

41% of girls have worn totally inappropriate clothes for an occasion!

CUTE PJS!

I was at a garage sale with my mom and found a cute shirt from one of the stores I love. I decided to wear it to school the next day and was super excited about it until a classmate came up and said, "I have those pajamas too!" I was so embarrassed and never wore that shirt again!

—Halli, age 11, Mass.

Your Sister's Fave Bracelet—Lost!

You borrowed your sister's charm bracelet for your first day of school. (And you got compliments on it all day!) But once you get home, the bracelet is gone. It's flown off your wrist like some kind of crazy magic bracelet! Or, maybe you just...lost it. Okay, don't panic! All you have to do is replace the bracelet before your sis finds out it's gone, right? But then you remember: She bought the charms on vacation...in Italy!

First, do a thorough search for the bracelet—at home and at school. No good? You have to 'fess up. Tell your sister how sorry you are, and ask how you can make it up to her. Can you buy her a similar bracelet, or do her chores for a month? The consequences of telling the truth may be tough, but the consequences of lying or making up excuses will be tougher! Besides, if you blow this, you may never get access to your sister's amazing closet again!

DG Poll

63%

of girls have lost something they borrowed!

CHAPTER TWO

Socially So...
Not Cool

BFF in an Awful Outfit

The first day of middle school is stressful for lots of reasons: new classes, new teachers, new friends. And of course, planning the perfect first-day-of-school-outfit. You spend hours deciding what to wear, but when your BFF shows you her selection, you can tell she clearly missed the memo. (You know, the one that said, "Don't wear anything that looks like it's from your grandma's closet.") "Isn't it adorable?" she declares. "It's vintage!"

You know how you're never supposed to lie? Well this is one of those situations where you *need* to. What's worse—having a little white lie on your conscience, or hurting your BFF's feelings over something as superficial as a dress? Remember that looks aren't everything, and tell your friend that you admire her creativity and unique style. She definitely won't have to worry about anyone else having her outfit, except maybe a teacher.....

DG Poll

36%

of girls have lied to their BFF about how much they liked her outfit!

Got a Not-So-Great Gift

Admit it: Your favorite part of your birthday is getting presents. Tearing into all those brightly wrapped packages is fun, especially when you love what's inside! At your birthday sleepover, you get the best gifts, like a super cute skirt and some awesome earrings that will go with everything. You save the best for last—the present from your BFF. But when you open it, surprise! It's a big...animal encyclopedia?! So maybe you did mention something once about wanting to be a vet, but, um...hello! "Do you love it?" your BFF squeals.

Unfortunately, you're about to learn a lesson: It's not about the presents. Your BFF gave this to you because she thought you'd love it. In fact, she probably bought it specifically with the hope that you would absolutely adore it. Of course, she was way off the mark, but still—it came from the heart, so you have to thank her graciously. No need to go over the top screaming, "Oooh! I've always wanted this!" A simple, "Thank you so much!" from your heart will do fine.

DG Poll

52% of girls have gotten a gift from a BFF that was so horrible they didn't know what to say.

Embarrassed by Dad

Your basement has everything: a big TV, a ping-pong table, and tons of video games. You love the fact that all your friends love to come over and hang out. But one day, your dad decides to ruin all that in the span of, oh, five minutes. He plops down on the couch and starts telling your friends stories about when you were little—including the time you peed your pants in your uncle's living room. Great.

Sometimes it seems like there's a rule that if you're a parent, you have to embarrass your kids. But try to remember that even though *you* see your parent's behavior as embarrassing, your friends probably don't. They might even admire the fact that your dad wants to get to know them! Most important, if you laugh at your dad, your friends are sure to laugh with you. Come back with something light like, "Yeah, that was hilarious! But not as funny as when you had to clean it up!" And then, very gently, tell him it was fun chatting with him, but you'll have to catch up more later. Much later.

DG Poll

74% of girls have been embarrassed by their moms or dads.

DADDY DEAREST

"The first day I bought a bra was a big day for me. I ran around the whole house bragging to my parents and younger sister. Later that night, my dad took me to youth group. The leader asked if anyone had anything special to share, and in front of the whole group, my dad said, "I'm so proud of my daughter who is growing into a young lady and wearing her first bra." Then the leader made all the kids come up and hug me! I'm never telling my dad anything again!"

—Sophie, age 12, Mass.

Forgot Lines Onstage

After years of landing non-speaking roles, you finally snag the role of Annie at your local theater. Yay! You've never been so incredibly happy to be an orphan! Not only that, but a reporter from your local newspaper will be in the audience on opening night! This could totally be your big break! But on opening night, you walk on stage, the music begins, and...you totally blank out.

Don't panic. If there's no one backstage ready to whisper your lines to you in an emergency (like this!) you're going to have to just make something up. You know the story and your character, so just go with it. Soon the director will figure out what's going on, someone will step in to save you, and you'll be back on track in no time. (And you can console yourself with the fact that every actress needs to know how to improv, and you just did!)

DG Poll

23%

of girls have gotten stage fright so badly they forgot their lines!

#9

You're Crushing...He's Not

This is it: you've decided to tell your crush you like him. You're sick of just watching him from across the cafeteria (and you already have his lunch schedule memorized—pizza on Mondays, bag lunch on Tuesdays...). So after psyching yourself up all week, you walk up to him and say, "I like you." Now he'll say he likes you back, right? But he just gives you a blank stare and says, "Uh..."

Finish quickly with, "You know, as a friend. And a bunch of us are hanging out this weekend, so I thought you might want to come." You'll cover up your confession, making it sound like your plan all along was to invite him to some group outing. (Note: If there is no group outing, organize one STAT!) Also, keep your cool—don't act any differently around him. Maybe your crush just needs time to get to know you, or maybe he was just shocked when you put him on the spot. Either way, give yourself major kudos for having the guts to put yourself out there.

NOT-SO-SECRET CRUSH

"I was at a school dance with my friends, and my crush was dancing near us. I just *had* to tell my friends how cute he looked, but the music was so loud they couldn't hear me. I repeated myself, louder and louder each time, but they still couldn't hear me. Finally I screamed, "I think Marshall looks super cute, but don't tell!" The song stopped right at that moment, so *everyone* heard me!

–Lindsay, age 12, Conn.

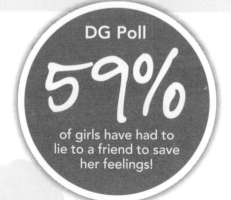

Caught in a Lie

Your friend calls you on Saturday afternoon and asks if you want to sleep over. That sounds like fun, but you already made plans to go to a birthday party you know she wasn't invited to. You don't want to hurt her feelings, so you tell her you're sick and even fake a cough for good measure. But the next day your mom happens to be talking to her mom, and she finds out that you were just fine!

Tell your friend that you *did* want to sleep over, but you already had plans. Let her know how much fun you always have at her house, and that you wanted to make sure you were invited again. Apologize for making up an excuse, and then, before she can say anything else, ask her if she wants to sleep over at your house next weekend. After a little bonding time, the two of you will be good as new.

#10

DG Poll

59%

of girls have had to
lie to a friend to save
her feelings!

Homework?! What Homework?!

You're sitting in math class, thinking about how boring algebra is and how you'll probably never use it in real life anyway, when the teacher says she's about to collect last night's homework. At first you think she's mistaken. There was no homework last night! But as your classmates start rummaging through their binders, you realize *you're* the one who's mistaken...and (uh-oh) you have no homework to hand in.

There's really nothing you can do, so stay calm. Most likely your teacher already has a policy for late assignments. You might get a zero, or you might just have points taken off if you hand it in the next day. Either way, explain the situation to your teacher, and just be honest. No matter what her policy is, she'll appreciate your maturity in handling the matter. Besides, it's highly unlikely that she'll believe the whole my-dog-ate-my-homework story!

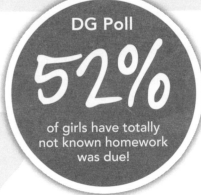

DG Poll

52%

of girls have totally not known homework was due!

Called Someone by the Wrong Name

You tend to get distracted in science because you have a perfect view of your crush, Tyler. One day when Tyler looks particularly cute, your teacher, Miss Stevens, asks you what a sedimentary rock is. You totally know the answer, but when you start to speak, you call Miss Stevens "Tyler"! Everyone laughs, and Tyler turns and looks at you like you've *totally* lost your mind.

This is super embarrassing, but here's the thing: By the end of the day, no one's going to remember this but you. Laugh it off and apologize with something like, "Oh, I'm sorry, Miss Stevens. I stayed up late last night and I'm just not thinking this morning." Then turn to your crush and pretend you need to ask him a question with something like, "Yeah, Tyler, I've been meaning to ask you about the homework. Did you understand the third question?"

BYE-BYE BLUNDER

"My family was on vacation and we ran into some old friends that we hadn't seen for a long time. As we were leaving after catching up with them, I shouted, "Bye Mr. and Mrs. Young!" It turns out Mr. Young wasn't Mr. Young at all! He was Mrs. Young's new boyfriend! They just stared at us... and I was so embarrassed!"

—Sara, age 10, Miss.

Broke Something Big

While your friend Emily runs to the bathroom, you start searching through her closet, looking for the perfect outfit for the party you're going to later. You spot *exactly* what you need: a super cute sparkly skirt! You whip it out...and accidentally knock over the lamp on your friend's desk. It goes crashing to the floor and breaks into a million pieces. To make matters worse, you know the lamp once belonged to her grandmother and is definitely an antique! Uh-oh!

You may be tempted to pick up the pieces, shove them into the trashcan, and slap an innocent look on your face. ("Broken lamp? What broken lamp?") Don't. When you make a mistake like this, it's much better to just come clean. The broken lamp will be discovered—and who's going to believe it threw itself off the desk? Tell Emily you understand the lamp probably can't be replaced, but you'd like to try anyway. She'll respect you in the end for being so honest...and you won't have to deal with a guilty conscience.

DG Poll

41% of girls have accidentally broken something that belonged to their best friend!

CHAPTER THREE

Body Blunders

#14

Farted in Front of Everyone

Your entire school is crowded into the gym for an assembly. When it's time to start, the principal tells everyone to quiet down. It takes a while but when everyone is finally settled, you accidentally let loose a big stinky one! Eww. You hear the girl behind you say, "Someone farted!" as people start turning to look at you...

This can be a big problem or a small mishap—it all depends on you. Don't try to blame it on someone else or say something like, "Whoever smelt it, dealt it." That'll draw even more attention to you, and besides, people will see right through your defensiveness. The best thing to do is to remain calm, pretend nothing happened, and keep your attention focused on the assembly. Soon everyone will forget about it and turn their attention to something else.

STINKY SCENARIO

"I was sitting next to my crush at school, and I felt really sick. I leaned over to tell my friend I wasn't feeling well when I accidentally let a giant fart slip out right in the direction of my crush! It smelled horrible, and the whole class was coughing and gagging! I tried to act like it wasn't me, but everyone knew. And now my crush avoids sitting next to me!"

–Lauren, age 11, N.H.

65% of girls have farted in a crowd!

Sweat Stains on *You!*

You're totally proud of the way you played in today's soccer game. You scored two goals and had an awesome defensive play against a girl twice your size. But as you're walking back to the locker room, your good mood is dashed when your friend says, "Hey, you have huge wet marks on your shirt!" You look down to see two dark stains by your armpits. At first, you're confused (how did you spill water all over your jersey?), but then you realize they're sweat marks! That's never, ever happened before.

Don't worry! This is totally normal, especially when you're pushing your body so hard. Try to just shake it off, and tell your friend that it must mean this was an extra-tough game. Before your next game, though, make sure you wear deodorant. Might as well keep it stashed in your gym bag so you'll never have to worry about forgetting it before a game!

DG Poll

41%

of girls have been embarrassed by underarm sweat stains!

SWEAT STAINS!

One day, I wore my favorite sweater with a tee underneath. The high school was having a musical and middle school students could participate. I was an Indian, which involved a lot of dancing. I got really hot, so I took off the sweater. We had to jump in the air with our arms up, and when it was my turn, I lifted my arms, and my armpits were completely covered in sweat and yellow stains! All the cool high school students were there and saw everything!

–Jamie, age 12, Tex.

Chocolate...on Your Pants

Could life get any sweeter? Your crush sat at your lunch table, and you've spent the entire period talking. (You have so much in common!) When the bell rings, he says, "We should sit together again tomorrow." "Okay," you reply, playing it cool. But when you stand up, you realize you sat on someone's chocolate bar—and now there's a huge brown stain all over the back of your pants. Gross. Your crush looks down and says, "What is *that*?"

Here's your chance to show your crush you're the kind of girl who can handle anything. Laugh it off, saying, "Oh, yuck— I sat on someone's chocolate bar! Excuse me—I'd better go wash it off." Don't freak out—just keep playing it cool. You probably won't be able to get the stain out, so if you can, tie a sweatshirt around your waist to hide it. You don't want to have to keep explaining what happened, because you have better things to do—like thinking about how fab it is to have a new lunch mate!

UNLUCKY FALL

"I was in the cafeteria, sitting next to my health-nut BFF, when she spilled her tomato juice. I ran to get napkins, but as I was coming back, I ran straight into my crush! Shocked, I stumbled back...and slipped on the tomato juice! To make matters worse, I fell right on my rear end, giving my pants a bright red spot! I had to walk around with that stain for the rest of the day!"

–Victoria, age 11, Vt.

45% of girls have sat in chocolate—or something else that looked really, really gross!

#17

Period on Your Pants

You're sitting in math, thinking about all the fun plans you have with your friends this weekend, when you get a weird feeling in your stomach. You rush to the girls' room and into a stall...only to discover that you've got your period! And if that's not bad enough, it leaked through onto your pants.

Stay calm. This is a major bummer, but it happens to *every* girl at some point in time. If you have a pad or a tampon, use it. (It's a good idea to always have one in your purse or locker.) If you don't, improvise by making a temporary pad from toilet paper or even (really!) a sock. If there's blood on your pants, try to blot as much out with toilet paper as you can, then tie a sweatshirt around your waist or see if any of your friends has a change of clothing you can borrow. Don't be afraid to head down to the nurse for help. Yeah, it might be a little embarrassing, but trust us—she's seen way worse.

DG Poll

20% of girls have had a period stain on their pants!

Slept in—on a School Day

Every night you remove your favorite silver necklace, put your hair into a ponytail, and set your alarm. Every single night. In fact, you haven't forgotten to set your alarm once this year, a streak you're totally proud of. But when the power goes out, your memory doesn't help. Your alarm clock is flashing two in the morning, but it's actually 8:00 a.m. And your bus comes at 8:05. Uh-oh.

It's all about prioritizing. You're not going to have time to watch your favorite cartoon or have homemade pancakes with whipped cream today. Instead, stick to the essentials—brush your teeth, throw on some (clean!) clothes, grab a granola bar, and get to the bus stop! Ideally, you should be planning ahead for days like this (just in case!) by laying out your clothes the night before. Also, grab a small mirror, hairbrush, and lip gloss on your way out the door so you can use the time on the bus to finish getting ready.

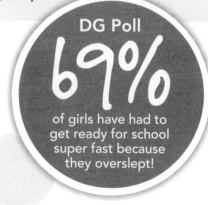

DG Poll

69%

of girls have had to get ready for school super fast because they overslept!

Oh, No! No Deo!

It's the morning of your big debate in social studies, and you can't wait to dominate the podium. You're going up against Dylan, this guy in your class who thinks he's smarter than everyone. But Dylan doesn't know what he's in for—you spent all night memorizing statistics and facts! Bring it on! But as you step off the bus, you realize that you forgot to put on deodorant!

Do you have some deodorant in your locker or gym locker? (If not, consider this a reminder to keep some there from now on!) Time to improvise. If none of your friends have any you can borrow, see if you can borrow some perfume or body spray to use on your pits. You can also run to the bathroom during the day and dab your armpits with a wet paper towel and some soap. Try to avoid a lot of physical activity that might make you sweat—this is *not* the time to showcase your new 50-yard dash time in gym! And don't let Dylan psych you out and make you sweat…because you're *totally* going to win the debate.

DG Poll

71%

of girls have forgotten to put on deodorant!

Slipped...and Everyone Saw!

Your sister forgot to wake you up and now you have just one minute to get to the bus stop. You grab your coat and sneakers, and dash down the icy sidewalk. But just as the bus pulls up, you slip rather spectacularly. Your skirt flies up and exposes your undies, and of course, all the kids on the bus see it all!

If ever you needed a sense of humor, it's now! As long as you're truly not hurt, just stand up and take a bow! Or say something like, "*Oooh*, that was graceful! I should be a ballerina!" And next time, even if you're in a rush, try not to run when it's snowing or icy out. You don't want to take a chance that you might *really* get hurt!

SLIPPERY ICE!

"My girls' hockey team was playing in a professional stadium. My coach told me to play center. As I skated over, I slipped and fell, sliding across the ice. Then I collided with the ref, and he fell on top of me! His face was pressed against my face, and we hit the boards. Everyone started laughing! Worst of all, when I looked up, I realized I was on the big screen!"

–Lesley, age 11, N.J.

Sneezed During Your Presentation

You've practiced your oral presentation on the Civil War what seems like a billion times—for your mom, your dad, your sister, and even your dog. When the big day arrives, you're totally prepared. But right when you start, you feel a sneeze coming on. You lift up your hands and—*achooo*! When you move your hands, there's snot all over them! Yuck!

Sneezing in front of the class is not a big deal, as long as you can keep your grace under pressure. Just say "excuse me," and calmly step away to grab a tissue. Wipe off your nose and hands, and then continue with your presentation as if nothing happened. Sneezing is normal, and it's no big deal to stop for a tissue. Chances are, people weren't even close enough to see what happened. By the end of the day, you'll have forgotten it happened—especially when you see you aced your presentation!

DG Poll

43% of girls have had a sneeze that was not well timed!

AHH-CH...EWW!

It was a cold winter, and I'd been recovering from a cold. On my first day back at school after missing three days, I still felt pretty crummy. My nose was running really badly, so I went to get a tissue. All of a sudden, I sneezed and a huge snot bubble came out and popped right on my face! I turned around in disgust, and my crush was standing right behind me! He laughed and asked, "Do you need another tissue?" So embarrassing!

–Abby, age 10, Maine

Sick at School

You know that nightmare where you're in class, and all of a sudden you get a queasy feeling in your stomach? Well, one Tuesday afternoon, that nightmare becomes reality! Before you know it, you're throwing up in the middle of science class. *Eww!* All your classmates turn to look, and some even run outside or plug their noses. So now you don't feel well *and* you're completely humiliated!

This is *not* the first time someone has thrown up in school. Everyone can probably remember a time when someone threw up in class—but they probably *can't* remember who it was, which is good news for you. People do understand that you can't help being sick. If anyone gives you a hard time, they're just immature. Laugh it off: "Yeah, that was gross! Being sick stinks." In a few days, your nightmare day will be a distant memory!

DG Poll

28%

of girls have thrown up in class!

THROW UP MESS UP!

"My best friend and I had to sing the school song at an assembly in front of everyone. My legs were shaky and I started sweating because I was so nervous! My friend was singing well, but I just stood there! Then all of a sudden I threw up...all over my friend's shoes! Everyone was laughing, but I was crying! It was a really awful day!

—Ally, age 11, Va.

CHAPTER FOUR

The Friendship Funk

First to Wear a Bra

Over the past few months, you've developed at what seems like the speed of sound. No big deal—you've started wearing a bra. (Your mom was actually really cool about it—she took you shopping for bras, which turned into shopping for *clothes*. Yay!) But since none of your friends are developed enough to wear a bra, you've felt weird about mentioning it. But now you have to change for gym, and that means changing into a sports bra...in the locker room. In front of everyone!

It's hard to be the first one to do *anything*, and wearing a bra is no exception. You can be proud of your maturity, and just put on your sports bra like it's no big deal. If *you* don't make a big deal about it, probably no one else will, either. However, if you can't bring yourself to change in front of everyone, just head to one of the bathroom stalls and change in private. Before long, everyone will catch up to you, and no one will give your sports bra a second thought!

DG Poll

43%

of girls have been embarrassed by wearing a bra before someone else.

#24

Friend Spilled Your Secret

You have a *super* huge crush on Matt, the new boy at school, but you haven't told *anybody*...well, except your BFF. But one day, a kid in your Spanish class pokes you in the side and says, "So I heard you like the new boy!" How could your friend have told?!

Yes, your friend may have told your secret, but you need to find out exactly what happened. Was it an accident? Did someone else find out and blab? Before calling your BFF a backstabber, make sure you get the facts. Then calmly ask her what happened. Next, deal with the issue: Everyone now knows you have a crush on Matt. While it might be embarrassing for you right now, in a few days everyone will have moved on to the newest piece of gossip and forgotten about your crush. (And on the bright side, maybe Matt likes you back but was too scared to say so!)

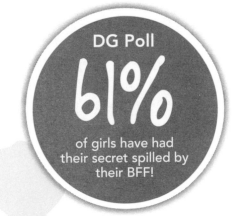

DG Poll

61%

of girls have had their secret spilled by their BFF!

SECRET'S OUT!

"My BFFs and I were sitting at lunch one day when the lunch monitor—who happens to be my crush's mom—walked up to us. Suddenly one of my friends pointed at me and blurted out, "She likes your son!" His mom said, "Sorry, he's too young to have a girlfriend." My friends all burst out laughing, and my face turned bright red! As if that wasn't bad enough, her son walked by and his mom said, "Honey, did you know she likes you?" I ran to the bathroom until lunch ended!

—Sam, age 9, Wash.

#25

You Made the Team, Your Friends Didn't

You and your friends have been practicing all week for volleyball tryouts. On the big day, everything goes according to plan: You ace your serve, and your friends all do an amazing job, too. Afterwards, you're waiting in the gym to find out who made the team. When the coach calls your name, you do one of those totally dorky jump-in-the-air fist pumps. But your good mood is soon deflated. *None* of your friends make the cut!

Eek! This is one of those situations where you feel like you're being torn in two. You're really proud of yourself...but how can you celebrate when your friends look so miserable? The most important thing is to be mindful of your friends' feelings. Congratulate them on their efforts, and remind them that there are other teams they can try out for. Be prepared for them to be a little bit jealous, and wait until you get home before celebrating. You can even tell your parents how humble you were, and make them feel totally obligated to celebrate with you even more!

DG Poll

36% of girls have made a team when their friends didn't.

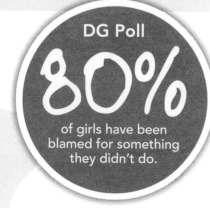

You Didn't Do It!

You're sitting on the couch watching TV when your mom calls you into the kitchen. She says that your friend Molly's mom just called to tell her that you made up rumors about her daughter...and now Molly wants to talk to you! Shocked, you tell her you'd never do that—it must be some sort of mistake! But she won't believe you, and says she doesn't want to hang out with you anymore. Friendship over.

Okay, so this is totally unfair and she's just plain wrong. Do *not*, we repeat, do not tell her what you think of her and her lousy accusation. Just calmly stick to the facts: You're sorry about what happened, but you didn't do it. You wouldn't do it. End of story. Don't argue, though—if Molly and her mom have already made up their minds, you won't convince them. The next day at school, try making your case again to Molly. Chances are that if you can convince Molly that you didn't make up the rumors, Molly can convince her mom as well.

DG Poll

80%

of girls have been blamed for something they didn't do.

#27

Best Friend...
Bad Hairstyle

You know those movies where the shy, quiet girl gets asked to the big dance by the most popular guy in school? Well it totally just happened to you! (Okay, so he's not the most popular guy in school, but he is really cute!) On the big night, your best friend comes over to do your hair. "It's going to look just like this," she says, pointing to a pic in a magazine. But once she's finished, it looks more like a nest than a hairstyle.

You can't wear a hideous hairstyle to the dance—you'd be completely self-conscious all night! But you *do* have to handle this carefully. Gently steer your BFF in another direction. Say something like, "Wow! It's cute, but I think it would be even cuter if we took out the clips and pulled it up more here." Before long, you'll have fixed the hairstyle—together—without her even realizing you hated it!

DG Poll

22%

of girls have gotten a not-so-great hairstyle from their BFF.

A CUTE CLOWN?

"My best friend and I were so excited for the school dance! I wanted to look super cute so I picked out my favorite outfit and my friend said she could do my hair. Turns out she had no clue what she was doing...my hair looked horrible! And she burnt it with the curling iron! I looked like a clown but I didn't want to hurt her feelings, so I went to the dance and tried to hide in the corner all night! So embarrassing!"

–Kristina, age 12, Fla.

Blurted Out a Bad Comment

You're having lunch with your friends, and the talk of the table is last night's school talent show. Your friends are going on and on about the skit they performed. (It was some kind of musical number, with a lot of dancing and jumping around.) Honestly, you thought it was kind of dumb, but you would never say that. Until... um...you do, when you accidentally let it slip that you weren't too impressed with their theatrical debut.

Time to backpedal! If the conversation is lighthearted, try throwing in a, "Just kidding! Of *course* it was fabulous! I was totally jealous that I couldn't be in it." Hopefully everyone will laugh it off. If they're not buying it or if this kind of remark would seem totally out of place, you're going to have to suck it up and apologize. Hopefully they'll be able to overlook your temporary lapse in judgment. (The same way you overlooked *theirs* when they wore those orange feather costumes last night.)

DG Poll

64% of girls have accidentally blurted out a mean comment!

AGING INSULT

"It was my teacher's birthday, and my class was trying to guess how old she was. "I bet you're 41!" one kid shouted. "No way!" I said. "She's not *that* old!" But it turned out that my teacher was 41. I had just called her "old"...right to her face! I was mortified!"

—Liz, age 9, Mont.

You Spilled a Secret

Your BFF announces that she's totally crushing on Danny, the cutest boy in your grade. You aren't really that surprised—who isn't in love with Danny? She makes you promise not to tell, and of course you agree. But the next day at school, you're talking to your other BFF and you accidentally let it slip. Oops!

You're not going to like what you have to do. Ready? Tell your friend what happened. We know it's hard, but if she finds out some other way—and she probably will—she'll be even *more* upset. If you're up front and honest, she's less likely to be angry with you. (Plus, you won't have to walk around afraid that she's going to find out.) Be prepared, though—she might be super mad, and it may take her a while to calm down. Just be extra nice to her—and maybe even let her borrow your cute pink dress that she's always admired. She'll get over it...eventually.

DG Poll

35%

of girls have spilled one of their BFF's secrets!

CHAPTER FIVE

Can't We All Just Get Along?

#30

Surprise Party Oops

You're throwing your BFF a surprise party. After finding the perfect cake and sending out the super-secret invitations, everything is set! Too bad you and your friends can't contain your excitement! You're talking about it at lunch when your BFF walks up, and you all instantly fall silent. "What are you talking about?" she asks. "Nothing," you quickly reply. "Right. Whatever," she says and storms off, thinking everyone was gossiping about *her*.

Sure, it's totally unfair, but even though your friend is annoyed now, she will be *so* excited on the day of the surprise. In the meantime, try to make up a little white lie, like "We were talking about Jen's crush and he was right there—that's why we all got quiet all of a sudden." Your BFF should get over it quickly, and you can explain what *really* happened at her party!

DG Poll

32%

of girls have had to bluff to keep a friend's surprise party a secret!

#31

No Dating Allowed

You're sitting in class when Justin, the boy you've been crushing on *forever*, walks up to your desk. He looks nervous, which makes you nervous. "Hey," he says. "I was just wondering if you'd like to go to a movie with me on Saturday?" Oh. My. Gosh. You've been asked on your first date ever! Too bad your mom said you can't date until high school...

Tell Justin you have to check with your parents first. Then, talk to your mom. Tell her in a really (*really*) nice way what happened. Is there any way she'd be willing to let you go? What if you make it a group date, or if she meets Justin and his parents beforehand? Would she feel better if you invited him to watch a DVD at your house? If you present all the options in a mature way, you might reach a compromise. But if she doesn't budge, explain to Justin that you tried, but your parents won't let you date until you're older. And don't worry—you *will* get asked out again.

DG Poll

14% of girls have had to turn down a date because their parents said they were too young.

Parents Don't Like Your New Friend

Everyone loves new friends, right? So when you start hanging out with Roxanne, you're sure your parents will be psyched. Sure, she's from another school, and no one *really* knows her, but you're sure she's sweet behind all that goth jewelry. But after you invite her over for dinner, your mom pulls you aside and says, "I don't want you hanging out with Roxanne again!"

Before you freak out, put yourself in your mom's shoes (even if they are totally out of style). She's probably not trying to be mean—she just wants to protect you. Try to figure out why she wouldn't want you hanging with Roxanne. Is she a bit more "mature" than you first thought? Is she always doing things you don't approve of? If not, and your mom is flipping out just because Roxanne is lacking table manners or dresses a little, uh, differently, have a talk about it. Explain how important this friendship is to you. (And the next time you have Roxanne over, it may be best to tell her to leave the goth jewelry at home.)

DG Poll

37% of girls have had a new friend their parents didn't like.

Invited to the Party...Late

Your on-again, off-again friend Katie is having a really cool birthday party. On the day she's handing out invitations, you wait for yours to appear in your locker. But at the end of the day, all you see are books and gym sneakers. When another friend asks if you're going, you admit you weren't invited. Then, two days before the party, Katie comes up to you and practically throws you an invitation. You *totally* know it was because she had to.

Okay, here's the thing: Whether or not she invited you because she "had" to or not, you have been invited. (Besides, why not assume the best? Maybe Katie meant to include you all along, but forgot to add your name to her list or temporarily misplaced your invitation.) The point is, this is a party you *really* wanted to go to, and now you're invited! Don't create unnecessary trouble—just go and have a good time with your friends!

DG Poll

26%

of girls have been invited to a party later than everybody else!

Stuck During Your Friend's Family Fight

You're at your friend Allie's house, leafing through the latest issue of *Discovery Girls* when, all of a sudden, the door to Allie's room flies open. Her mom bursts in and starts yelling at Allie about a bad grade she received. Yeah, it was a D, but still—this is *way* over the top! Allie's trying to talk to her mom, her mom's flipping out, and you...well, you're sitting there, wondering what to do.

Can you say "uncomfortable"? Yikes! Allie's mom should have respected the fact that Allie had a friend over and saved the scolding for later. But since Allie and her mom don't seem to realize this, it's time for you to hit the road. Tell them you think it might be better if you came back when things have calmed down and silently slip out of the room. The last thing this fight needs is someone in the middle of it.

DG Poll

42% of girls have been stuck in the middle of a friend's family fight.

GET ME OUT OF HERE!

"I was hanging out at my friend's house after school. When her dad got home from work, he started yelling at her that she was still grounded and was not supposed to have friends over! I didn't know what to do so I called my mom to pick me up, but we live 15 minutes away so it took her awhile to show up. I had to sit there the whole time, listening to them argue and wishing I could get out of there!"

—Rose, age 8, Iowa

Regret a Comment

There's a new girl at school, and you decide to take her under your wing. Yay for new friends! You spend lunch talking about how you love pizza, old movies, and how you absolutely can't stand the latest pop star that everyone else seems to be crazy about. The conversation must be a success, because she invites you to sleep over that weekend. But when you get to her bedroom, surprise! She has posters of that same pop star *all* over her walls.

Yikes! While it may be slightly uncomfortable to realize you made fun of her fave star, she probably doesn't even remember. If she does bring it up, say something like, "Yeah, I don't really care for him, but your room looks great! I love the color of your walls!" The most important thing is to let your new bud know that just because you don't like that music doesn't mean that you don't like *her*!

DG Poll

69%

of girls have accidentally made fun of something a new friend loved!

NOT REALLY RUDE!

"I was at a store with my older sister. My sister calls me "young one" (because I'm younger than she is), and I call her "old one." As we were leaving the store, I said, "Hurry up, old one!" What I didn't realize was that an old lady was walking by. She thought I had called her old and told her to hurry. I was mortified! I'll never call my sister that in public again!"

–Daniella, age 11, Ariz.

Invite...or Not?

You finally got your parents to let you have a party at the *amazing* country club in town. You can't wait to hit the pool and order those yummy sandwiches. But before you can say, "fiesta," Mom and Dad decide you can only invite four people. And to make things even worse, one of your not-so-close friends sees you passing out invitations. "What's the deal?" she asks, hand on her hip. "How come I'm not invited?"

Here's a great rule: *Never* pass out invitations at school. Never! Put in a little extra effort and either mail or email them. That way, you avoid this whole scene. Of course, everyone will probably still find out who was invited—and who wasn't. Nicely explain to those you couldn't invite that your parents would only let you invite a few people. And keep the "My-party's-going-to-be-so-awesome" talk to a minimum. (Of course it is—but you don't have to make the people who weren't invited feel even worse.)

39% of girls have had to limit a guest list for their party and leave out a friend.

Overheard Gossip— About You

You're in the locker room after volleyball practice when you hear a few girls talking on the other side of the lockers. The conversation sounds juicy, and you just can't help but listen in. "She's so annoying," one of the girls says. "Totally," someone replies. You bet they're talking about Kristy, this girl who always moves away from the ball because she's scared of it. But then you realize...they're not talking about Kristy at all—they're talking about *you*!

Okay, this hurts, and there's really no good way to fix it. You can't make people like you, and confronting them might just make it worse. Remember that these girls are *not* your friends, and honestly, you wouldn't *want* them to be. Chances are, if they're gossiping about you, they're also gossiping about each other. So after a breezy, "Bye, girls!" go home and call your BFF. She'll remind you of the awesome, true friends you have by your side, and you'll be able to forget about those gossipy girls.

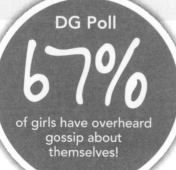

DG Poll

67%

of girls have overheard gossip about themselves!

Crush Confusion

You're sitting in the cafeteria when Carl Hodge sits down next to you. You've been avoiding him all week, since it's rumored that he likes you, and you're totally not interested. You pretend you don't see him (la la la), but he doesn't budge. "So," he begins, and you know what's coming. "Look," you say. "I know you're going to ask me to the dance but I don't plan on going." "Uh," he says, looking confused. "I just wanted to know if you could loan me a few bucks for a sandwich." Oh.

Talk about embarrassing! The only way out of this one is to apologize. Tell Carl you're sorry, and that you shouldn't have assumed he was asking you to the dance. Then loan him some money and send him on his way. And next time, try not to take the words out of people's mouths! They might just surprise you.

DG Poll

38%

of girls have thought a boy was about to confess a crush...but he wasn't!

CRUSHED BY CRUSH

"I have a crush on my best friend's brother, and at her house one day I heard him telling a friend on the phone that he liked me! I was so excited! The next day at school I went up to him and said, "I just want you to know that I like you too!" He said, "What? I like the other Cara!" I was so embarrassed and my best friend will not let me live it down!"

—Cara, age 11, Ala.

Accidentally Used A Racist Term

You've been hearing a new rap song on the radio lately, and it contains a word you've never heard before. It's on the radio, so you figure it's just some harmless slang. But when you start singing the song while riding to a softball game with your friend's family, your friend's father turns around and says, "What did you say? That's a terrible word—it's very racist."

As anyone who has ever been teased knows, words *can* hurt, and racial slurs are as bad as it gets. So even though you didn't mean any harm, you need to apologize. Tell your friend's father that you had no idea the word was offensive, and that you were just singing a song you'd heard on the radio. Then thank him for letting you know it's not something you should be repeating. There's a lesson here: Find out what a word means *before* you use it!

DG Poll

54% of girls have unknowingly said a word that turned out to be offensive or racist!

CHAPTER SIX

Pressure! Pressure! Pressure!

Tempted to Cheat

You've enjoyed a string of A's and A+'s in math since, like, kindergarten. You're struggling through this quarter, though, and when it's time for the final test, you know you have to ace it or your average will be ruined. You study and study, but on the day of the test, you're still pretty nervous. Right before it starts, your classmate pokes you. "Hey," she says from the seat next to you. "Check it out." And then she opens her binder and shows you a copy of the answer sheet. "You want a copy?"

You most definitely do not! Cheating is *never* a good idea. Chances are you'll get caught. Not to mention, you'll feel super-guilty afterwards. And are you really going to be happy about your grade if you know you got it by cheating? Your classmate won't be angry if you want to take the test on your own, and if she is, she's not someone you want to hang out with anyway. Turn the offer down, and do your best on the test...without the answer key.

DG Poll

87% of girls have been tempted to cheat but resisted.

Party? Parents Say "No"!

Your BFF is throwing a boy/girl birthday party, and you're super excited! But unfortunately, your parents totally nix your plans. They don't approve of boys being there! You're miserable, but your BFF is totally unsympathetic. "Best friends come to each other's parties," she says. *"No matter what."*

First, remember this isn't about your mom vs. your BFF. It's about your mom trying to look out for you, and your BFF really wanting you to be there. Talk to your mom. Is there a way to make her feel better about the party? Can your BFF's mom reassure her that the party will be well chaperoned? If she won't give in, don't pitch a fit. Instead, explain to your BFF that you're just as upset as she is. If possible, plan a special day together to make up for it. When your BFF sees that you really do care, she'll get over the fact that you're going to miss her party.

DG Poll

47%

of girls have had to miss a party because their parents wouldn't let them go!

Cyberbullied

You're checking your e-mail while eating your after-noon snack (apples with peanut butter, mmm), when you see something that makes you stop mid-bite. A "friend" has sent you an angry e-mail, and she says some pretty nasty things. First you're shocked...and then you're super mad. How dare she! Maybe you should e-mail her back with a piece of your mind!

One problem with the Internet is that it makes it *way* too easy to fire off a few choice words when you're angry—before you have time to cool down or consider the consequences. Remember, there's a real person on the other end of that computer. If you're not willing to say something in person, don't put it in an IM or e-mail. Feeling angry? Step away from the keyboard. That way, you won't type something you'll regret. (Especially since everything can be printed out for parents to read. Can you type G-R-O-U-N-D-E-D?)

DG Poll

33% of girls have fired off a mean comment online because they were angry.

Easy A...or No Way?

After social studies, your teacher pulls you aside and says, "I just wanted to tell you what a great job you did on the Cherokee project! You must have worked so hard, and you definitely deserve the A+ I've given you!" Oh, fab! Except, um, you haven't turned in that project yet—you accidentally left it at home. She must have mistaken another student's A+ project for yours!

You can't take credit for something you didn't do. Sure, it's tempting, but that grade belongs to someone else. Plus, the mix-up will more than likely get sorted out, and then your teacher will wonder why you took the credit. So 'fess up and tell the truth—your teacher will respect your honesty, and you won't have to walk around on eggshells waiting to be found out.

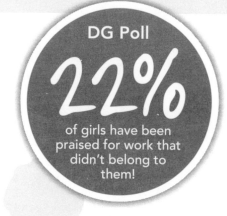

DG Poll

22%

of girls have been praised for work that didn't belong to them!

Asked Out, and You Need Out

The rumor mill at school is in full force: Word is you're about to get asked to the spring dance! Too bad the guy who's going to ask you isn't exactly crushworthy. (His special talent is making fart noises with his armpit.) You try to avoid Armpit Boy, but it's impossible. It's a small school and he's determined. He finally corners you by your locker and pops the question.

Careful! This has to be handled delicately. Remind yourself that—armpit noises aside—this guy does have feelings, and you don't want to hurt them. Besides, you have to give him credit—it takes a lot of guts to ask someone out! So be kind but firm. Say something like, "I'm really flattered, but I can't—I have other plans that night." Or—if you can make this happen—use your friends as an excuse: "I'm really sorry, but my friends and I are all going in a group. Girls only." There *are* nice ways to say no!

ROSES AND ROSY CHEEKS

"There was a really nice but dorky boy in my class who had a big crush on me. On Valentine's Day, my friends and I were at lunch when he came up and gave me a huge bouquet of roses and a giant teddy bear that wouldn't even fit in my locker! He asked me to go out with him, but I told him we should talk about it later since everyone in the lunchroom was looking! Talk about embarrassing!"

—Sara, age 10, Miss.

DG Poll

38% of girls have turned down a boy because they didn't return the feeling.

Pressured by Your Mom

Your school is creating the first-ever field hockey team for girls. Yawn. You've never been one for sports, but your mom has a different opinion. She was the all-star goalie on her high school field hockey team, and she's decided you're going to follow in her footsteps. "How fun!" she says, holding up two pairs of cleats. "I didn't know which ones you'd like, so I got both!"

Okay, so the thought of playing field hockey is about as appealing to you as a trip to the dentist. But that's probably just because it's something new and scary. Is there any way you could make field hockey fun? Maybe ask some of your friends to join with you? If you really don't want to play, talk to your mom. Make sure you let her know what you'll be doing instead, whether it's writing for the school newspaper or joining the debate team. If you politely explain that her dreams are not *your* dreams, she's sure to understand.

DG Poll

42%

of girls have had to tell their parents they're not interested in the same activities as their mom or dad.

CHEERFUL CHAOS!

My mom was a cheerleader in high school and has always wanted me to be one, too. I decided to try out for the squad to make my mom proud, and she was so excited on the day of tryouts. I'd been practicing my routine for weeks, but I managed to mess up the whole thing! The worst part was all my friends were there to cheer me on! At least my mom realized that cheerleading was her thing and not mine that day!

–Caroline, age 12, Nev.

Mean Teammate

During a soccer game, your teammate, Casey, accidentally kicks the ball out of bounds in the last 30 seconds of the game. Soon after, the team snob, Megan, charges over with her friends and says to Casey, "It's your fault we lost! You totally blew it!" Then Megan turns to you and says, "Don't you agree?"

Standing up to Megan might seem like dooming your social life forever, but if you let Megan get away with putting Casey down, she could turn on *you* next. (And when we say "could" we mean "will." Girls this mean usually end up turning on everyone at some point!) So stand up for yourself and Casey. Just say, "The loss really lies in all of our hands, not just Casey's. If we'd all played harder, it wouldn't have ended up so close." Chances are, the other girls will agree and back you up. And without the support of her friends, Megan will be powerless. *And* she'll think twice the next time she tries to push someone around!

DG Poll

73%

of girls have stood up to a mean girl to defend their friend.

CHAPTER SEVEN

Mysterious Messages

Unknown Screen Name

You're sitting at the computer, putting the finishing touches on an English essay that's due tomorrow (and by "finishing touches," we mean, you know, just starting), when an unknown screen name pops up in your IM window. "Who is this?" you type, hoping it's the boy from your church who's rumored to have a crush on you. But the person starts acting all mysterious, claiming to know you, even though you have no idea who it is.

You should never, *ever* talk to someone online unless you know them, since you can easily end up in a dangerous situation without even realizing it. The Internet can be very deceptive—it can seem safe even when it's not. The person behind the screen name may not be who he (or she) is claiming to be—you never really know who's on the other side of the computer. Your best bet? Only chat with people you know in "real life." And if you ever receive IM-s from a stranger or e-mails that make you uncomfortable, tell your parents ASAP.

DG Poll

33% of girls have had a stranger talk to them online.

#48

Approached by a Stranger

You're shooting hoops in your driveway, when a man you don't recognize approaches you and asks if you've seen his lost puppy. "This is him," he says, flashing a pic of a super cute golden retriever. "Can you help me find him? I don't really know the neighborhood, and it will only take a second." You want to help, but you are worried about the fact that he's a stranger.

You *should* be worried that this guy is a stranger! Never go off with someone you don't know, no matter what the reason. Tell the guy no, and then head inside. Immediately tell your parents or another trusted adult. This guy may be up to no good, and it's better that you let someone older deal with it.

DG Poll

19%

of girls have had a stranger ask them for help.

Cornered by a Scary Dog

You're walking through the park when this cute dog you've never seen before starts to approach you. Aw. You love dogs! "Hey, boy," you say softly, holding out your hand. "Where did you come from?" But then he growls, suddenly looking more killer than cuddly, and starts moving toward you...

Your first instinct may be to turn and run—*don't*. Running will just make the dog want to chase you. Instead, show him that you aren't a threat by keeping your arms at your sides and standing still, even if he comes closer to sniff you. Don't make eye contact or smile at him. (He may think you're baring your teeth.) Most likely the dog will lose interest in you and leave. But if he sticks around, wait for signs that he's decided you're okay: His growling has stopped, the fur on the back of his neck is down, and his ears are up. Then *slowly* back away.

DOWN, DOGGIE!

"I had to go to a party with my mom one night at her friend's house. When we got there this friend had a huge dog. I had to go to the bathroom, so I went upstairs and the dog followed me! He wouldn't stop barking and growling at me and I started crying and wouldn't leave the bathroom! I'm still embarrassed!"

—*Ellen, age 13, Ky.*

58% of girls have been cornered by a terrifying dog!

Home Alone, Stranger Knocks

You're home alone, working on your dance moves, when the doorbell rings. You hear a man yell, "UPS! I've got a package I need you to sign for!" Yay! You've been waiting for some stuff your mom ordered over the Internet. You know you're not supposed to answer the door when you're home alone, but it's the UPS man! What would it hurt, just this once...?

Stop! Never answer the door when you're alone. For anyone. Even if you think the person on your doorstep is just a delivery man or a neighbor, it's better to play it safe. If it is a delivery man, he'll probably leave a slip to be signed and bring the package back the next day. He'll also get back in his truck and be on his merry way in a few minutes. If the person hangs around or tries to convince you to open the door, call your parents or another trusted adult and let them know what's going on.

DG Poll

64%

of girls have had to ignore someone at the door when they were home alone.

SCAREDY CAT!

'My parents went on a date one night, and I stayed home watching my little brother. We were watching movies and it was really late when someone knocked on the door! I was so scared. I turned off all the lights and made my brother hide in the closet. Then I heard my dad's voice yelling from outside. It was just my parents wanting me to let them in since they forgot their keys. They still make fun of me for being so scared!'

–Marissa, age 12, Ohio

A Weapon...at School

You're at your locker, grabbing your stuff for gym class, when you hear the boy whose locker is next to yours bragging to his friends that he's going to bring a weapon to school tomorrow! You can't tell if he's joking or not, and all the noise in the hall drowns out the rest of the conversation. You head to gym, unsure what to do. He was probably just joking...right?

There is only one thing to do in this situation: *Tell an adult immediately.* Even joking about bringing a weapon to school is not okay—they're dangerous (*duh*!). Maybe the kid is just fooling around, but what if he isn't? If anything happened, you'd never forgive yourself. Tell a teacher now.

DG Poll

25%

of girls have overheard somebody threatening to bring a weapon to school!

Mystery Phone Caller

You're home alone on a Sunday night, watching a movie, when the phone rings. You figure it's your BFF, calling for your traditional end-of-the-weekend gab session. "Hello?" you say, settling in for a nice long chat. But it's not your BFF. "Hi, this is your dad's friend from work, Bob." Bob? You've never heard of him. You grab a pen and get ready to take a message. "Actually," Bob says, "I just need your home address so that I can send your dad some important papers. It would be great if you could just give it to me."

Is this guy for real? Look, you don't know him. Even if you *have* heard your dad talk about someone named Bob, it's *never* a good idea to give your address or any other personal information out over the phone. Tell him your dad is busy (never say you're home alone) and that if he gives you his number, your dad will call him back soon. If it turns out Bob really is who he says he is, both he and your dad will understand. In fact, they'll be proud of you for being so smart.

DG Poll

15% of girls have had a stranger call while they were home alone and ask for personal information.

#53

Threatened by Class Bully

The class bully was making fun of your friend's new braces in math class, calling her things like "braceface" and "metalmouth." (Couldn't he come up with something more original?) "Don't even worry about that jerk," you tell your BFF. But what you don't realize is that the bully is standing right behind you! "I'll be waiting outside for you after school," he growls. He's a lot bigger than you and could hurt you if he wanted to...you're in trouble!

Bullies like this are super dangerous—physical violence is not okay in any circumstance. You need to tell a teacher, pronto. Sure, you don't want to come off as a tattletale, but trust us, anyone who thinks like that isn't worth your time. This is one of those instances where you have to just suck it up and do the right thing—before you or someone else gets hurt.

DG Poll

44%

of girls have stood up to a class bully by telling an adult!

CHAPTER EIGHT

Stuck!

Lost in the Woods

It's your first time ever camping at Mt. Shasta. It's so cool—you love the smell of the campfires and the trees, and you can't wait to check the area out. You decide to just go a little way into the woods to explore, maybe pick a few wildflowers...but before you know it, you're totally lost.

Don't take a chance that you'll get even farther from the campsite: Find a big tree or a large rock, sit down, and stay put. (Remember, though, you want to find a resting place, not a hiding place.) If you're with your dog, sibling, or friend, *stay together*. Got a whistle? Three toots indicates distress. Otherwise, sing (it's easier on your vocal chords than yelling) or bang rocks together to help rescuers find you. If you have something white or brightly colored (a bandana, a piece of paper) make sure it's visible. If you're not found by nightfall, cover yourself with leaves to help you stay warm. Most important, don't panic—your parents are probably looking for you already!

DG Poll

21% of girls have been lost in the woods!

Hiding a Big Secret

Your dad lost his job a few months ago, and your family had to move from your huge house to a smaller one. You were kind of embarrassed, so you never told your friends what was up. "Hey," your friend says one day when you guys are hanging out at the park. "How come we never hang out at your house anymore?" "Yeah," someone else says. "Why can't we come over?"

Living in a smaller house is nothing to be ashamed of, but it's totally understandable that it's hard to tell your friends your dad lost his job. Unless you're *never* going to have friends over again, at some point you're going to have to come clean about your new digs. How much you reveal, though, is up to you. Maybe you just want to tell your closest friends what happened. Or maybe you don't want to tell anyone. If your friends ask why you moved, you could just say your parents wanted a smaller house, and leave it at that.

DG Poll

14%

of girls have had to keep a secret about why they moved.

SPLIT SECRET

"My parents were getting a divorce and I hadn't told any of my friends yet, but my older brother had told his friend...who had then told one of my friends. At recess one day, that friend asked if it was true and I was so caught off guard and embarrassed! I turned bright red and ran off crying! I wish I'd have told my friends in the first place because they just wanted to help!"

–Stephanie, age 10, Calif.

#56

Shoplifting Friend

You're in your favorite clothing store with a friend, trying on clothes and having a blast. But once you're out of the store with your purchases, your friend pulls a necklace out of her pocket. "Hey," you say. "Did you...did you steal that?" "Shhh!" she says, fastening it around her neck. "Don't worry, it's just a necklace."

Eek! This girl needs a wake-up call before she ends up in deep trouble! Tell her you're not going to hang out with her anymore if she's going to shoplift, and if she ever does it again, you're going to tell your parents. This is going to put a major crimp in your friendship—she's not likely to throw her arms around you and thank you for your concern. But what if she gets caught the next time you're shopping together? You could *both* end up being charged with stealing. It's so not worth it...no matter how close you two are.

DG Poll

12%

of girls have had to tell a friend to stop shoplifting!

Pressured by a Friend

You _really_ want to spend the night at your friend Carrie's house, but your mom says no because she doesn't know Carrie's parents. So you tell a teeny lie, and say you're spending the night at your BFF's instead. But then Carrie starts daring you to do things you _know_ are wrong, even dangerous. You just want to go home, but if you call your mom, she'll totally know you lied.

So now you know that lying to your parents was a really bad idea, but too late for that now—you're already there. A friend should _never_ pressure you into doing something you don't want to do. Tell Carrie that if she keeps it up, you _will_ call your mom. If she doesn't stop, you're going to have to follow through. While you might get in trouble, dealing with the punishment is much better than staying in a weird or dangerous situation. And if you point out to your mom that you did the responsible thing by calling her even though you knew she'd be mad, she might go a little easier on you.

DG Poll

55% of girls have had to tell their parents the truth after lying to get out of a situation gone bad!

Forced to Choose Between Divorced Parents

Your parents are getting divorced (*ugh*) and they still don't know which one you're going to live with (*double ugh*). You're totally bummed—you hate not knowing what's going to happen. And then, just when you think things can't get any worse, your parents say they have to talk to you about the living arrangements. They sit you down and ask *you* to choose!

Choosing between parents is a horrible position to be in. How can you even begin to think about choosing between your mom and your dad? If there's any possible way, try to work out a compromise. Can you switch between the two houses? Live with one parent but visit the other frequently? Take into consideration the practical aspects of one house versus the other. For instance, would you have to switch schools? And is one of your parents better equipped to take care of you? If you really can't decide, tell them that while you're glad they trust you enough to make your own decision, you really need their help on this one.

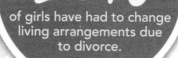

DG Poll

26%

of girls have had to change living arrangements due to divorce.

Stranded Without a Ride

After a long Saturday at the mall with your BFF, you head to the main doors to wait for your parents to pick you up. But when your BFF leaves with her big brother (who just got his license), you're stuck waiting alone. Bor-ing. After watching car after car drive by, you're getting antsy. It's been 20 minutes since your friend left, and your ride still isn't here. You'd call home, but you don't have a cell phone.

Go back inside the mall and head into a store, restaurant, or kiosk. Ask if you can use the phone. (You can also look for a pay phone, but stay in well-lit areas where there are people around.) If everything is closed, find a security guard to help you. In the future, make a pact with your friend that if you're getting separate rides, you'll wait for each other to get picked up before taking off. And if you've been begging your parents to get you a cell phone for "emergencies only," now's the perfect time to make your case!

DG Poll

62% of girls have been stuck somewhere waiting for a ride.

Walked in on Parents...Naked

You just got home from spending the night at your friend's house, where you put that dye in your hair that washes out after three shampoos. You can't wait to freak your parents out with your new look...pink hair is totally you! You run upstairs to show them, but when you push open the door to their room, they're...*naked*!

Your first instinct is probably to yell "Gross!" while running down the hall. But resist that impulse—really. Just close the door quickly and walk calmly to your room. (And, no—once there, don't IM everyone you know, saying, "OMG, I just walked in on my parents naked!") Your mom or dad might come to talk to you about what happened, or they might decide to pretend it never happened. Either way, they're probably embarrassed, too, so stay calm and let them know you can handle this maturely.

DG Poll

67%

of girls have walked in on their mom or dad when they were undressed!

#61

Caught Cheating

It's the night before the big Spanish test, and you haven't learned any of your vocab. Figuring it's a lost cause, you go to bed without studying. The next day, as you're taking the test, you discover you can easily see your neighbor's paper...and she always gets A's. You know it's wrong but it's just this once! But before you can turn in the test and make a clean getaway, your teacher notices your wandering eyes, calls you over, and rips up your test!

You made a mistake. It happens. What you did was wrong and no doubt you're going to feel guilty about it. There's really nothing you can do now but apologize to your teacher, tell her you know you made a huge mistake, and spend the rest of the year trying to earn back her respect and trust. How, you ask? By always being prepared for class, remembering to study for tests, and being a responsible student. If you truly are sorry and don't do it again, you'll be back on track in no time!

DG Poll

17%

of girls have been caught cheating!

CHAPTER NINE

Rescue Team

Locked Out

After a long day of hanging out at your BFF's house, you hop on your bike and head home. But when you get there, your house is locked. Thank goodness you know where your key is...too bad it's inside on your dresser, where you left it this morning. No one is home, and you can't go back to your friend's house, because she already left for dance class!

Ideally, you should make a plan with your parents so you'll know what to do if this happens. (Perhaps you can even hide a key outside.) If it's too late for that, think hard. Is there a back window open? Can you get in through the garage? If not, you'll just have to hang out until someone comes home. If it's going to be a super long time, head to the house of a neighbor you trust and ask if you can call your parents. Never go inside your neighbors' house if you don't know them, though—ask them to bring the phone outside to you, or to call for you. And next time, make sure you have your key before you take off.

DG Poll

65% of girls have been locked out of their house!

Runaway Pet

You love walking your cute little dog, Monster. Okay, so it doesn't hurt that your crush lives close by, and it gives you an excuse to go by his house! One afternoon, as you and Monster are on your fifth trip around the block, he yanks on the leash and goes running down the street. "Monster!" you yell. But he won't stop...and he's running into a busy intersection!

Stop! Chasing Monster will probably just make him run faster, and it might put you in danger. Stay calm and check out the situation. If there's a green light for pedestrians and you can grab Monster or his leash, do so—*carefully*. But if the street is way too busy, find an adult who can help. From now on, be a little more cautious, and hold onto that leash!

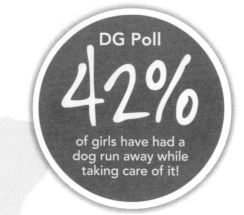

DG Poll

42%

of girls have had a dog run away while taking care of it!

House Fire

You're in a totally awesome mood—you're sitting on your bed reading, enjoying a bowl of ice cream topped with your special homemade hot fudge sauce. Yum! But your great mood goes up in flames when you smell smoke coming from the other side of your door!

Uh-oh. Is it possible you forgot to turn off the stove? No matter what, stay calm. If anyone else is home, yell, "Fire!" to alert them to what's going on. Feel your door with the back of your hand. If it's hot, it's best not to open it. Try escaping through a window instead. If this isn't an option and you must go through the door, crawl out, staying low to avoid inhaling smoke. Once you're out of the house, run to a neighbor's to call 911. And if your clothing ever catches fire, remember: *Stop, drop, and roll!*

DG Poll

16%

of girls have been involved in a house fire!

Microwave in Flames

You're babysitting for the kids next door, and when it's time for lunch, they want hot dogs. So you open the package, wrap a few in aluminum foil, and pop them in the microwave. You're patting yourself on the back for being such a great babysitter...when you realize there's a fire inside the microwave!

First, a word to the wise: *Never* put aluminum foil or any kind of metal in the microwave. Never. (Unfortunately, you just learned this the hard way—oops!) Do *not* open the microwave door. Doing so will only make the fire worse. Instead, leave the door closed—the fire will run out of air and burn itself out. If you can, unplug the microwave, then get yourself and the kids out of the house, and call the fire department from a neighbor's house.

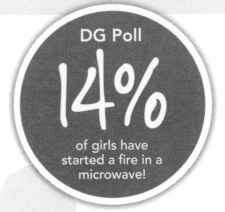

DG Poll

14%

of girls have started a fire in a microwave!

Injured Animal

You're walking home from school one day when you hear a weird chirping noise. You look down to see an injured bird lying in the middle of the street! He's so cute, and it looks like he can be saved if you just pull the stick out of his wing. "Hi, little birdie," you say, crouching down. He flutters his wing helplessly. There are cars coming, and you don't want him to get hurt...

While it's tempting to help, you should never, ever touch an animal you don't know—especially a wild animal! Birds in particular are known to carry diseases that can infect humans. And although you may think you're helping, you could end up hurting the poor bird even worse. The best way to help him is to hurry home and ask an adult to call your town's animal control center to pick the bird up. You'll stay safe, and the bird will have a better chance of recovery in the hands of professionals.

DG Poll

26% of girls have alerted the authorities about an injured animal.

Tornado Warning

Your parents are out for the night, and you and your little sis have the house to yourselves. You're sitting around, watching TV, when a special bulletin comes on. At first, you're totally annoyed that they're interrupting your favorite show, but your annoyance turns to panic when the announcer says there's a tornado coming. Suddenly, you hear thunder and lightning, and the lights start to flicker...

Don't panic—just do what you need to do to stay safe. If you have a basement or underground cellar, take your little sis down there and wait until the storm passes. If you don't have a basement, stay on the lowest floor of your house. Keep away from windows, and, if possible, take cover in a bathroom or closet, or get under a sturdy table or doorway to protect yourself from falling debris. Stay put until the storm has passed.

DG Poll

30%

of girls have felt threatened by a big storm while home alone!

Why Are Friendships So Confusing?

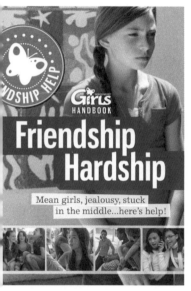

SHE KNOWS EVERYTHING about you...she'd never tell your secrets...she's your biggest fan. Who doesn't want a friend like that?

True friendship is a gift... but it can be hard to find. Whether you're stuck in a fading friendship, caught in the popularity trap, or dealing with mean girls, we'll break down the solutions to your problems step by step. Best of all, we'll teach you how to free yourself from poisonous friendships forever and be the best friend you can be.

Soon, you'll be meeting new people and making friends who truly respect and understand you...because you deserve first-rate friendships.

When Did Life Get So Complicated?

Sᴛᴜᴄᴋ ʙᴇᴛᴡᴇᴇɴ ꜰʀɪᴇɴᴅꜱ? Tired of your siblings? Self-conscious about your body? Crushing big time?

You're not alone. Every month, girls write to *Discovery Girls* magazine to ask Ali, our advice columnist, for help with issues like these.

When it comes to girls' most troublesome questions, Ali has all the answers you need. She tackles your questions on everything from family to friendship to school to boys...and much, much more.

No matter what you're going through, you'll find answers to your problems inside. Ali is here to help!

Getting Over Bad Days

My Worst Day
...and How I Survived It

Inspiring Stories from Girls Who Have
Overcome Tough Times

AUBRIE'S BEST FRIEND TOLD HER they couldn't be friends anymore because Aubrie was "too weird" to be seen with. Torrie was so upset when her parents divorced, she gained 20 pounds and let her grades go into freefall. Mackenzie watched her mom grow sicker and sicker and then die, just when Mackenzie needed her most.

In these amazing true stories, girls just like you share their private struggles, hoping to help you through your most difficult times.

You'll find comfort, encouragement, and inspiration here...and best of all, you'll know that whatever life throws at you, you are never alone.

Look for this and other bestselling titles at DiscoveryGirls.com
ISBN 978-1-934766-07-1
$9.95